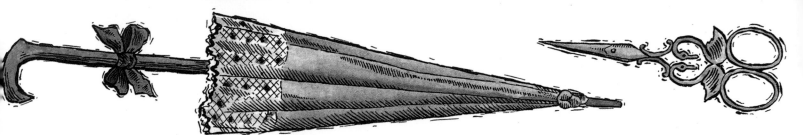

WHAT·DO·WE·KNOW
ABOUT  THE
VICTORIANS·?

RICHARD TAMES

MACDONALD YOUNG BOOKS

First Published in 1994
by Simon & Schuster Young Books
Reprinted and published
in paperback in 1997, 1998 and 1999
by Macdonald Young Books

Macdonald Young Books an
imprint of Wayland Publishers
Limited, 61 Western Road
Hove, East Sussex
BN3 1JD

You can find Macdonald Young
Books on the internet at
http://www.myb.co.uk

Designer and illustrator: Celia Hart
Commissioning editor: Debbie Fox
Copy editor: Jayne Booth
Picture research: Valerie Mulcahy
Series design: David West

Photograph acknowledgements: Front and back cover: Popperfoto; The Bridgeman
Art Library, pp16 (Harrogate Museums and Art Gallery), 17(t) (Royal Holloway and
Bedford New College, Surrey), 20(b) and 25(b) (Christopher Wood Gallery,
London), 43(tr) (private collection); The Thomas Cook Travel Archive, p41(b); The
Co-operative Union Ltd, p15(c); courtesy of the Dickens' House Museum, London,
p36(r); E.T. Archive, pp22(l), 23(b), 26(r) (Sir Benjamin Stone Collection), 39(b);
Mary Evans Picture Library, pp14(b), 20(t), 27(b), 36(l), 41(t); Fine Art
Photographs, pp9(t), 12(b) courtesy of Fine Art of Oakham, 21(t), 25(t) (N.R. Omell
Gallery, London); Fitzwilliam Museum, University of Cambridge, p40(l); Guy's
Hospital, London, Evelina Children's Hospital Appeal, p31(b), Hulton Deutsch
Collection, pp9(bl), 9(br), 17(b), 26(l), 33(t), 39(t); Leeds City Art Galleries, p34;
Manchester City Art Galleries, p23(t) *The Dinner Hour, Wigan* by Eyre Crowe; The
Mansell Collection, pp15(b), 19(t), 21(b), 33(b), 37(r), 38(r); William Morris
Gallery, endpapers; Museum of London, p14(t); courtesy of the Director, National
Army Museum London, p42; National Maritime Museum, London, p43(b); National
Portrait Gallery, London, pp15(t), 28, 32(l), 32(r); The National Trust Photographic
Library, p35(b) (Andreas von Einsiedel); The Natural History Museum, London,
p38(l); Florence Nightingale Museum, p30(b); The Robert Opie Collection, pp13(l),
13(r), 27(t), 30(t); Picturepoint, p43 (tl); Royal Academy of Arts, London, p35(t);
The Salvation Army, p29(b); Richard Tames, pp18(t), 22(r); Tate Gallery, London,
pp24, 29(t), 31(t), 37(l); TRIP, pp18(b) (Peter Rauter), 19(b) (Jim Watters);
University of Reading, Rural History Centre, p12(t); courtesy of the Trustees of the
V&A Museum, p8.
We are unable to trace the copyright holder of the Great Western Steamship poster
on p40(r) and would appreciate receiving any information that would enable us
to do so.

Printed in Hong Kong by
Wing King Tong

A CIP catalogue record for this book
is available from the British Library

ISBN: 0 7500 2459 3

Endpapers: This printed fabric was
designed by William Morris in1883,
it is called 'Strawberry Thief' (see page 35).

· CONTENTS ·

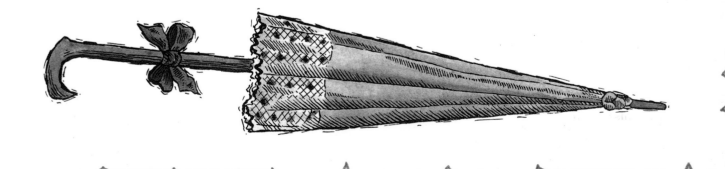

WHO·WERE·THE·VICTORIANS?

Queen Victoria reigned over Britain and its Empire from 1837 to 1901. Her 64 year reign was the longest in British history and is called the Victorian period after her. During Victoria's reign the British were immensely proud that they had the world's biggest Empire, largest navy and most modern industries. Educated people felt they were living through a time of exciting progress with new inventions making life better for everyone each year. But millions of Britons were still poorly fed, badly housed and often unable even to read or write.

BRITAIN ON SHOW

This painting shows the opening ceremony of the Great Exhibition of 1851, the first ever 'world fair'. It was held in London's Hyde Park in a huge glass and iron hall called the Crystal Palace. Over 6 million visitors came to see the new inventions, works of art and products from all over the world which were on show for six months. Victoria and her husband, Prince Albert, are standing on the platform.

 PENNY POST

Before railways were built, letters went by stage coach. The charge depended on the distance as well as the weight. Railway transport was so much cheaper that it became possible to charge the same whatever the distance. This is a 'Penny Black', the first sticky stamp to show the postage fee had been paid in advance.

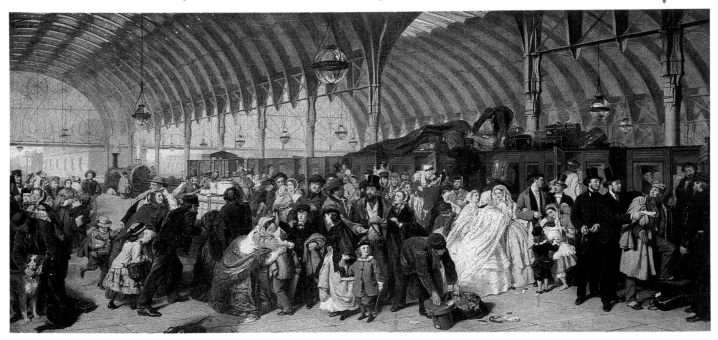

RAILWAY REVOLUTION

Victoria's reign was the great age of railway-building. Railway travel was four times faster and much cheaper than travel by horse.This painting by W.P. Frith (above) shows London's Paddington Station. The artist wanted to show all the different kinds of people who travelled by train. Luggage was piled onto the roof of the carriages and there was no cab to shelter the driver. Can you see two policemen arresting a man who is trying to get away?

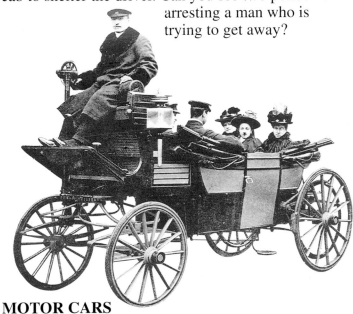

MOTOR CARS

Petrol-engine motor cars were invented in the 1880s but until the 1920s only rich people could afford them. They were called 'horse-less carriages' – and that's exactly what they looked like! This one had its engine under the driver's seat.

SLUMS

Almost every big city had areas of slum housing where the poorest people lived without proper lighting, heating and drainage. This engraving shows Irish immigrants in the East End of London in about 1870. Up to 40 people could live in one house!

TIMELINE

	1830–1840	1841–1850	1851–1860	1861–1870
BRITAIN	1830–7 Reign of King William IV. 1830 Liverpool–Manchester railway opened. 1832 First Reform Bill gives more middle-class people the vote. 1833 *Pickwick Papers* by Charles Dickens published. 1837 Victoria becomes Queen. First electric telegraph built. 1840 Penny postage introduced.	1842 Parliament bans employment of children and women underground. 1845–6 Famine in Ireland. 1846 Repeal of the Corn Laws which had limited imports of grain to keep prices up. 1847 *Wuthering Heights* by Emily Brontë published. 1848 First Public Health Act passed.	1851 Great Exhibition held in Hyde Park. 1852 Building of Houses of Parliament completed. 1856 Safety matches invented. 1859 *Origin of Species* by Charles Darwin published.	1863 World's first underground railway system opens in London. 1865 Salvation Army founded. 1866 Trans-Atlantic cable links Britain and America by telegraph. 1867 Working men in towns get the vote. **Houses of Parliament**
THE BRITISH EMPIRE	1833 Abolition of slavery in British Empire. Britain claims Falkland Islands. 1835–9 'Great Trek' by Boers to escape British rule in South Africa. 1835 Melbourne, Australia, founded. 1840 Wars against China and Afghanistan. 1840 Britain takes control of New Zealand.	1842 Britain takes control of Hong Kong.	1851 Gold rush in Australia. 1857–8 Rebellion against British rule in India crushed.	1867 Canada becomes self-governing. 1868 Last convicts sent to Australia.
EUROPE	1831 Polish revolt against Russian rule crushed. 1837 Crowns of Britain and Hanover separated. 1839 Belgium and Luxembourg become independent.	1848 Year of revolutions throughout Europe. Karl Marx and Friedrich Engels publish *The Communist Manifesto*.	1852 Napoleon III proclaimed Emperor of France. 1854–6 Crimean War – Russia defeated by Britain and France. 1854 First railway across the Alps.	1861 Serfdom abolished in Russia. 1863 Polish revolt against Russian rule crushed. 1864 Red Cross founded in Switzerland. 1867 Swedish chemist Nobel invents dynamite. 1870 Italy unified as one country. **Abraham Lincoln**
REST OF THE WORLD	1834 First mechanical reaping machine (USA). 1837 Morse code invented (USA). **Morse code**	1845 Texas joins the United States. 1846 First operation under anaesthetic (USA). 1846–8 War between USA and Mexico.	1851 Singer sewing-machine (USA). 1853 Levi jeans invented (USA). 1853 Japan forced to open to trade. 1859 First oil well drilled in Pennsylvania, USA.	1861–5 American Civil War. 1865 Assassination of President Abraham Lincoln. 1867 USA buys Alaska from Russia. 1869 Suez Canal opened. Railway links USA coast-to-coast.

1871–1880	1881–1890	1891–1900	1901–1910
1873 Lawn tennis invented. 1875 Major Public Health Act is passed. Captain Matthew Webb becomes first person to swim the English Channel. 1876 Queen Victoria becomes Empress of India. 1878 Joseph Swan invents light bulb. **Light bulb**	1882 First ship-load of chilled meat imported from Australia. 1883 *Treasure Island* by Robert Louis Stevenson published. 1884 Working men in the countryside get the vote. 1887 Victoria celebrates Golden Jubilee – 50 years as Queen. 1888 Pneumatic (air-filled) tyre invented. **Sherlock Holmes**	1894 Tower Bridge opened. 1897 Victoria celebrates Diamond Jubilee – 60 years as Queen. *Dracula* by Bram Stoker published. First *Sherlock Holmes* story published.	1901 Death of Queen Victoria. 1901–10 Reign of Edward VII. 1902 *Peter Rabbit* by Beatrix Potter published. 1904 *Peter Pan* by J.M.Barrie published. 1906 HMS Dreadnought – the most advanced battleship of its time – launched. 1908 Old-age pensions introduced.
1873 Ashanti war in West Africa. 1875 Britain takes control of Suez Canal. 1877 First cricket test match between England and Australia. 1879 Zulu war in South Africa.	1882 Britain takes control of Egypt. 1886 Gold discovered in South Africa. 1889 Colonisation of Rhodesia (Zimbabwe) begins.	1894 Britain takes control of Uganda. 1896–8 Britain reconquers the Sudan. 1897 Gold discovered in Canadian Klondyke. 1899–1902 Boer war in South Africa.	1901 Australian colonies united. 1907 New Zealand becomes self-governing. 1910 South African colonies united.
1871 Germany unified as one country. 1874 First exhibition of Impressionist paintings held in Paris. 1877–8 War between Russia and Turkey.	1885 Benz and Daimler make first motor cars. 1887–9 Eiffel Tower built in Paris. **Eiffel Tower**	1891–1903 Trans-Siberian Railway built across Russia. 1805 X-rays discovered. Moving pictures invented. Wireless invented. Tchaikovsky's *Swan Lake* first performed. 1896 First modern Olympic Games held in Athens. 1898 Zeppelin airship invented. First diesel motors used.	1901 First Nobel Prizes awarded. 1903 First 'Tour de France' cycling race. 1904 Anglo-French Entente – Britain and France oppose rising power of Germany. 1909 Frenchman Louis Blériot is the first person to fly across the English Channel.
1876 Alexander Graham Bell invents telephone in USA. Massacre of General Custer by Buffalo Indians at Little Big Horn. 1877 Edison invents phonograph. 1879 Edison perfects the light bulb.	1880–90 'Scramble for Africa' as European powers divide continent into colonies. 1886 Statue of Liberty erected in New York, USA. 1889 Slavery abolished in Brazil.	1894–5 War between China and Japan. 1898 War between USA and Spain. 1900 Boxer Rising in China. First hamburger produced in USA.	1903 Wright Brothers make first manned, powered aircraft flight in USA. 1904–5 War between Russia and Japan.

TOWARDS ONE WORLD

When Queen Victoria came to the throne in the 1830s it took 11 hours to go by stage coach from Bath to London, a journey of about 160 kilometres. By the 1860s the railways had cut the journey time to less than two hours. In the 1830s communication between Britain and America depended on the speed at which a ship could cross the Atlantic. A sailing ship might take six weeks, depending on the weather. In 1838, the steamship *Sirius* did it in 14 days. After 1866, Morse code messages could be sent across the Atlantic in seconds through a cable laid on the ocean bed. In 1897, Queen Victoria marked her Diamond Jubilee by sending a telegraph message from Buckingham Palace to Australia in under two minutes. In the same year an imperial penny postal service was introduced – send a postcard anywhere in the British Empire for one penny!

Cheaper, faster and more reliable travel and transport meant a huge increase in the movement of goods and peoples around the world. Tens of millions of people emigrated from Europe to find new lives overseas. Railways opened up vast areas of North and South America, South Africa, Australasia and Siberia to settlement and cultivation. Steamships enabled Westerners to penetrate central Africa and the Amazon. By 1900, only the Poles and highest mountains remained unvisited.

WHERE·DID·PEOPLE·GET·THEIR·FOOD?

Britain's population rose from 10.5 million in 1801 to 20.8 million in 1851 and 37 million by 1901. British farmers had to grow more and better food to keep up with rising demand, but as railways and steamships made it easier to bring meat and wheat from abroad, the country came to rely on imports for about a third of all its food. Half of Britain's people lived in towns by 1850, so more and more families had to get food from shops. In the country, people still relied on markets and their own vegetable gardens.

THE STEAM PLOUGH

The engraving above from around 1850 shows a crowd of well-dressed people watching a ploughing demonstration using steam engines instead of horses to pull the plough. The plough was dragged along wires stretched across the field. A company called Ransome's of Ipswich made these machines from 1854 onwards but they were too expensive for most farmers to buy.

THE COUNTRY MARKET

The painting to the right shows the market at Malmesbury, Wiltshire around 1860. Markets were still important in country areas. Buyers could see that the produce really was farm fresh – including live poultry! Wicker baskets were used both to transport goods and to display them.

ADVERTISING AND PACKAGING

Food manufacturers quickly realised that brightly coloured labels made their products look better. This mustard advertisement (right) boasts that the Queen uses Colman's. Because some shop-keepers cheated customers – for instance, by mixing tree-leaves in with tea-leaves – people began to prefer foodstuffs in sealed packets, like these below, which also helped to preserve them.

IMPORTED FOODS

The map below shows some of the many countries which exported food to Victorian Britain. Many of these food industries were started by British settlers from the 1870s onwards. There were no sheep in New Zealand or Australia before the British introduced them. British planters also started tea plantations in India and Sri Lanka. Before that all tea had come from China.

AMERICAN FOOD FADS

The United States pioneered many of today's convenience foods and snacks. These include doughnuts (1847), chewing gum and canned sweetcorn (1848), candy bars (1853), canned baked beans (1875), evaporated milk (1884), Coca-Cola (1886), Horlick's (1887) and cornflakes (1898). Crisps were invented in America in 1853 but didn't reach Britain until 1913, after an Englishman had seen them in France!

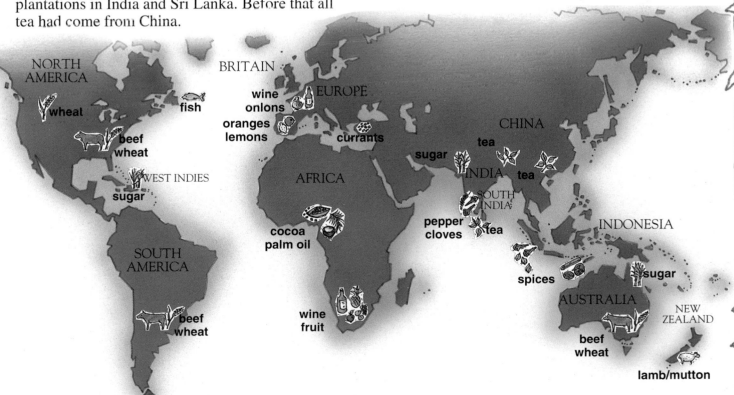

DID·PEOPLE EAT·WELL·IN VICTORIAN ·TIMES?·

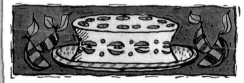

Foreign travel and the wider range of foods imported from abroad made rich people interested in trying out new dishes. British people who had lived in India spread a taste for dishes such as curry, spicy mulligatawny ('pepper water') soup and kedgeree, a rice and fish dish. But the poorest half of the population too often had to make do with tea, bread, jam, potatoes and bacon – a diet that did not give children the nutrients they needed to grow strong. Gas cookers were invented in the 1830s but did not become common until the 1880s. The first slimming diet was published in 1862!

A COFFEE STALL

This painting shows a coffee stall in London in about 1850. The lady on the right is drinking one-handed while clinging on to her hat-box. The boy on the barrow has poured his coffee in a saucer to cool. The badge on his sleeve shows that he is a street-sweeper for the City of London. Other street stalls sold hot pies, pastries or roast chestnuts. Not everyone had cooking facilities at home, so stalls like these provided the only hot food some people ever had. Stalls were cheap but not always very clean!

THE BAKE-HOUSE QUEUE

In industrial areas where many women went out to work it was difficult for them to cook hot meals for their families. So they took a joint of meat or a stew to a bake-house in the morning and collected it, cooked, on the way home. Left-overs could be reheated or eaten cold for a second meal. From the 1860s onwards it became possible to buy freshly fried 'fish and chips' in most industrial towns because the railways could bring fish, packed in ice, from the coast before it went off. 'Chips' were invented in France, which is why they are called 'French fries' in the USA. Fish and chips were wrapped in old newspapers and often eaten straight away with the fingers.

A DINNER PARTY

This painting was done in 1884 and shows dessert being served at Haddo House in Scotland. It is a very grand occasion, with a Highland piper playing and lots of silverware on the table. The hostess, with her back to us, is the Marchioness of Aberdeen. She is talking to the guest of honour, the Prime Minister, William Gladstone. At such formal dinners all the men wore tail-coats and white ties and the women wore silk evening gowns.

TABLEWARE

Wealthy people used different kinds of cutlery and crockery for each dish. Most of the cutlery was made in Sheffield and the crockery around Stoke-on-Trent. The moustache cup shown below was designed to lift whiskers clear when drinking tea or coffee.

Moustache cup

Egg cups and spoons on a stand

Sandwich servers

THE CO-OP

The Co-operative movement was started in Rochdale, Lancashire in 1844. It aimed to help poorer people beat cheating shop-keepers by selling basic goods cheaply. Each year, instead of keeping any profit, it would pay customers a 'dividend' on what they had spent.

SOUP KITCHENS

Soup kitchens, like the one on the right, were set up to give free food to homeless children or to adults when unemployment was particularly high. This engraving shows a bearded man and a lady with a hat giving out soup. Their good clothes show that they are well off. Such people thought that helping the poor was their Christian duty. Women with servants often filled their spare time working for charities.

Most families were large. In the 1850s the average farm labourer had seven children or more. By 1900, the number was down to five. In towns many families had a male lodger or two. It was very unusual for a single man with work to live alone and cook for himself. Most families were glad to have lodgers for the extra income they brought in. Wealthy families were also big. Rather than lodgers they often supported unmarried aunts or sisters. And a family of six or seven might well have that many servants living in as well to look after them.

Doll

A FAMILY OCCASION

Victorian people thought that family life was a great blessing. This painting of 1856 shows a birthday party in a middle-class family and is called 'Many Happy Returns of the Day'. The children have been given a glass of sherry as a special treat. Count how many children and ladies there are – the girl by the door is a servant. Grandfather is reading his newspaper.

Doll's house

HOME, SWEET HOME

This splendid doll's house shows what the home of a well-off middle-class family would have been like. Girls were given doll's houses because it was expected that one day every girl would stay at home as a wife and mother rather than go out to work. Boys might have been given a fort or a model farmyard to play with.

QUEUEING FOR SHELTER FOR THE NIGHT

When this painting was first shown at the Royal Academy in 1874 it shocked the well-off middle classes who saw it. These homeless people are queueing for free shelter for the night. You can see the policeman with a beard on the left. There is also a family (right) with four children, one of them barefoot. The mother is crying in despair.

 A SERVANT'S WORK

There were a million servants in Britain in 1851 and 90 per cent were female. The best-paid job for a woman was as a cook. She might earn £30 a year, plus a uniform, food and her own room. The worst job was scullery maid. She had to light the coal fires and wash the dishes. These recipes (right) show that many cleaning products were home-made. Most ladies' dresses couldn't be washed and had to be unmade and remade for every cleaning.

> **TO CLEAN SILK OR RIBBONS**
> Mix 300ml/1/2 pint gin, 225g/8oz honey and 225g/8oz soft soap with 300ml/1/2 pint water.
>
> **TO RESTORE WHITENESS TO SCORCHED LINEN**
> Boil 300ml/1/2 pint vinegar, 50g/2oz fuller's earth, 25g/1oz dried fowl's dung, 15g/1/2oz soap and the juice of 2 large onions.

ORPHAN CHILDREN

Desperate parents sometimes deserted their children but most orphans had lost their mother and father through accidents or diseases such as cholera or typhoid. Sometimes orphans were sent to factories as cheap labour and were treated badly. The picture above shows an orphanage at a meal-time. The girls and boys are separated and are all wearing uniforms. At bedtime, the children slept in dormitories. When they grew up most orphan girls became servants. Boys were often sent to sea.

WHAT·SORT OF·HOUSES DID·PEOPLE ·LIVE·IN?·

Until the coming of railways the great expense of transporting building materials meant that most houses were built from whatever was available nearby. This usually meant buildings blended in with the landscape. Railways made transport so much cheaper that red bricks and Welsh roof-slates could be used in almost any part of the country. The new areas of towns began to look more and more alike, with long streets of identical homes. By 1900, most town streets had proper pavements and lighting while new homes had gas lighting and drainage, if not an inside lavatory.

A GENTLEMAN'S HOME
This engraving of a country house of the 1830s shows how most English people would have liked to live – surrounded by lovely gardens and grounds, with plenty of space for riding and entertaining friends. Fast railway travel made the weekend country house party popular with the upper classes. Guests would come from the towns to enjoy shooting and hunting during the daytime and dining, cards and dancing in the evenings.

A COAL MINER'S COTTAGE
The living room of this Durham miner's home has a large range which is both a fire to heat the room and an oven to cook in. Above is a rack for hanging cloths to dry in the warm air. Miners usually got their coal free and burned a lot of it. As families became better off they liked to show their good fortune by filling their homes with ornaments like the china dogs in this room or the religious mottoes on the wall. There is also a lot of brass which was kept brightly polished. As machines replaced craftsmen in the factories, more and more goods for the home became affordable.

UNDER THE RAILWAY ARCHES

This engraving shows working-class housing in London in the 1870s. The houses look grim and dreary and the smoke from the railway overhead must have made the washing hung out in the back yards very dirty. But there are proper windows and drainpipes and each home has a scullery with a chimney sticking out at the back. This means the families could heat water in a 'copper' for washing and baths. Northern cities, like Leeds, had far worse slums with houses built 'back-to-back' so that the only windows were in front and there wasn't even a back yard. Almost everyone rented their homes in Victorian times.

NEW COMFORTS IN THE HOME

Gas lighting gave a better and cheaper light than candles, so more people stayed up in the evenings. Electric lighting was invented in the 1880s but was still rare outside central London and other big cities until after 1900. Ways of making cast iron cheaper meant more families could afford a mangle for squeezing hot water out of the washing. But only the middle classes had gadgets like coffee grinders. Devices like carpet sweepers were slower to become popular in Britain than in the USA, where they were usually invented. This was because the people who could afford them had servants, whereas in America more women did their own housework.

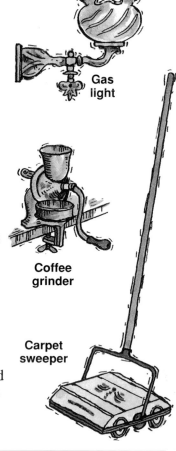

Gas light

Coffee grinder

Carpet sweeper

MANSION FLATS

In Scotland people had been used to living in multi-storey tenements since the 1600s, but well-off English people didn't like the idea of living without gardens. In the 1880s the first 'mansion flats' were built in London. They were attractive to wealthy people with small families or no children. They were also cheaper to heat and maintain than a whole house. These mansion flats are in Bedford Park, west London, which was the capital's first 'garden suburb', with lots of trees and flower beds. You can see the apartments have balconies for window boxes and face onto a lawn with rose-trees.

·DID·BOYS· AND·GIRLS ·GO·TO· SCHOOL?

Educated people were not at all sure that it was a good idea for *everyone* to learn to read and write. They thought that poor people should be able to read the Bible for themselves - but if they could read that they might want to read other things, like newspapers wanting reforms or supporting trade unions. But from 1833 onwards the government gave money to church-based charities which ran schools and from 1839 it appointed inspectors to see that they were doing their job properly. The government took over responsibility for education after 1870 and in 1880 made all children between the ages of five and ten go to school.

THE PUBLIC SCHOOLS
The rich sent their sons to 'public schools' which were in fact private. This is Rugby School (left) which set new standards by teaching French, maths and history as well as Latin and Greek. It also encouraged team sports and taught leadership to older boys by making them prefects. Better-off girls were often taught at home by a visiting teacher or live-in governess.

DAME SCHOOLS
This painting (right) shows the sort of school, run by a 'dame', which existed in most villages. She was usually a poor widow who ran her 'school' in her home to earn a few pennies. The children were all taught together and there were very few books or teaching aids and little equipment. This dame is teaching the children the alphabet. Very often she could do little more than read and write herself. Some dame schools were really just a child-minding service for working mothers. But many poor children never had the chance to go to any other kind of school.

BOARD SCHOOLS

This painting shows a 'board school' for children where there was no church or charity school available. Although the pupils are still all in one room there are two trained teachers and proper blackboards and desks. The younger children have slates to write on and older ones have paper.

BEHAVE YOURSELF!

Victorian teachers paid as much attention to good behaviour as they did to learning. Cheekiness and disobedience were punished by beating. Dunce's caps or sleeve badges like these were used to shame lazy, dirty and naughty children.

Sleeve badges

EDUCATION FOR ALL

Between 1833 and 1840, government spending on education had risen from £20,000 a year to £170,000. By 1860, the figure was over a million pounds and 4 million by 1880 and 12 million by 1900. By 1900, almost 90 per cent of children aged five to eleven were enrolled in a school. But the number actually at school was lower, especially in the countryside when there was work to be done in the fields. Only four children out of ten were at school between the ages of twelve and fourteen and only three in 100 after they were fourteen. Special schools for deaf and blind children were set up from 1893 onwards.

TEACHING BY PUPILS

The picture above shows a school run on the 'monitorial system'. This was a way of trying to make up for the shortage of trained teachers. The teacher would teach each lesson to a team of older pupils – the monitors. The monitors would then repeat the lesson to the younger pupils while the teacher was free to attend to particular children. You can see a monitor teaching the two-times table and another at a wall map teaching geography.

WHO·WENT TO·WORK·IN VICTORIAN ·TIMES?·

Although more people than ever before were going to work in mines and factories, traditional skills and crafts were still important. As late as 1851 there were more people making shoes and boots than mining coal. There were more tailors than seamen and almost twice as many women doing washing as men making iron. Making cotton and woollen cloth in factories often involved working with dangerous machines but at least it was indoors and dry. In mines and on farms whole families were often hired to work with the father acting as the children's boss. Very few workers got pensions so they worked until they were too old for anyone to employ them.

THE TRADE UNIONS

Trade unions, known as 'combinations', were banned by law between 1799 and 1824. Many were formed during the unrest of the 1830s and 1840s but most collapsed because they were badly led or their members were too poor to go on strike. The splendid membership certificate of the Amalgamated Society of Engineers (left) shows the pride of the highly skilled workmen. They were most successful in forming effective unions because often they could read and write and so they could keep proper written records and run their organisation efficiently. Only very skilled workers who had completed a seven-year apprenticeship could join the unions like this. They wanted to limit the supply of such skilled labour to protect their own jobs and keep their wages as high as possible. Some skilled workers earned as much as school teachers or shop-keepers. Unions of unskilled workers began in the 1880s.

DOWN ON THE FARM

When this photograph was taken around 1900, much farm work, like haymaking, was still done by hand and horse power despite the invention of steam-powered machinery. From the 1870s onwards, British farmers had to compete with cheap food from abroad. Farm wages fell and many labourers emigrated.

THE NEW WORLD OF WORK

This painting shows women workers outside the factories of Wigan, Lancashire in 1874. They are resting during their midday meal break. They have brought their food and drink with them because there were no factory canteens. The old woman bending over has been selling fresh milk in tins. The girl behind her is clearly able to read as she is looking intently at a letter. The women have tied back their long hair to stop it from getting caught in machinery. The tall chimneys are pouring smoke and smut into the air. There are gas lamps to light the way home at night.

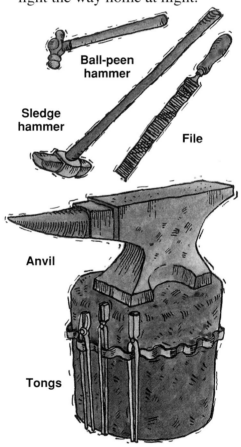

Ball-peen hammer

Sledge hammer

File

Anvil

Tongs

A BLACKSMITH'S TOOLS

In 1851, there were still over 120,000 blacksmiths at work in Britain. They were needed to repair farm tools and carts as well as to shoe horses and make wrought-iron gates.

 MEN'S WORK, WOMEN'S WORK

Many jobs were regarded as 'male' or 'female'. In 1851, farms employed most people – with seven men to every woman. In domestic service there were eight women to every man. In the cotton industry the numbers were about even but in building work there were over 440 men for every woman employed. In dress-making the difference was even bigger and the other way round – about 700 women for every man.

CHILDREN'S WORK

This photograph above shows a boy learning to make shoes around the year 1900. By then the worst treatment of children at work had been banned by law. At the start of Victoria's reign children of five or six had been sent down mines to operate ventilation doors, sent up chimneys to clean them and sent out to the fields to weed crops.

·WHAT·DID· PEOPLE·DO IN·THEIR ·SPARE· ·TIME·?·

During Victoria's reign amusements became less cruel and more organised. Tormenting bulls and bears with dogs for sport was banned by Parliament, though cock-fighting still went on in country barns and fox-hunting was more popular than ever. Railways made it possible for hunters to reach the Scottish Highlands to shoot deer and grouse. The growth of inter-school sports led to agreed rules for different games. Rugby split off from soccer. Bare-knuckle boxing changed to boxing with gloves in a limited number of rounds. In the towns, parks were provided for families to enjoy fresh air and flowers.

ON THE MOVE

The 'penny-farthing' bicycle (right) gave a splendid view but riders needed a good sense of balance as they were 1.5 metres off the ground! Cycling really became popular in the 1880s when the modern 'safety bicycle' was invented, fitted with air-filled rubber tyres for a soft, smooth ride.

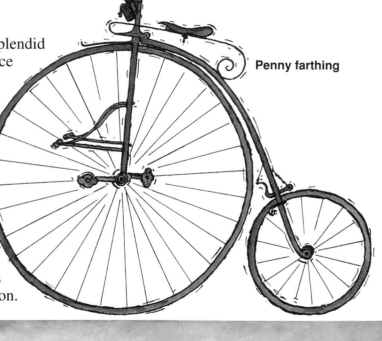

Penny farthing

DERBY DAY

This painting shows the huge crowds of both rich and poor gathered for England's most famous horse-race. On the right a kneeling coachman is spreading out a picnic. In the middle is an acrobat and next to him is a man with a big drum to get people's attention.

THE SEASIDE

This painting shows Brighton in the 1880s. The promenade and pier were built so that visitors could breathe fresh sea air without stumbling on sand or shingle. Invalids were often told to take a seaside holiday for their health. On the beach is a Punch and Judy show and a row of wheeled 'bathing machines' where people could change and jump straight into the sea. Railways made it much easier to get to the coast. Brighton was only an hour from London. Blackpool and other seaside resorts grew rapidly because of the railways. Even working people could afford a day trip.

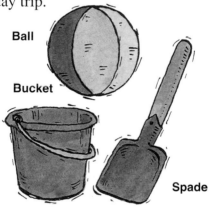

Ball

Bucket

Spade

A NEW GAME

Lawn tennis was invented in the 1870s. It was originally going to be called 'sphairistike'! It was an ideal game for the garden of a large middle-class house. As it was played rather gently, girls could join in, even though they wore lots of tight, heavy clothes. They also did archery and played croquet.

MILESTONES IN LEISURE

The first town park is laid out in Preston, Lancashire.	1834
The first swimming club is formed in London.	1837
Sussex forms the first County Cricket Club.	1839
The first British camera club is formed in Edinburgh.	1842
The first Rugby Football Club is formed at Guy's Hospital, London.	1843
The first amateur dramatic society is formed in Manchester.	1848
The first children's play ground is laid out in Manchester.	1859
The first athletics club is formed in London.	1863
The first international soccer match – England and Scotland draw 0–0.	1872
Snooker is invented at a British army officers' club in India.	1875
First Test match is played between England and Australia.	1877
Twelve clubs found the Football League.	1888
Volleyball is invented in the USA.	1895
The first modern Olympic games are held in Athens.	1896

· W H A T · DID · THE · VICTORIANS · WEAR ?

Victorian people wanted clothes that would last. The poor just had to make their clothes last and many bought second-hand clothes or wore cast-offs. But the rich wanted clothes that lasted to show that they could afford good quality. Well-off young ladies might follow the latest fashions eagerly, but this was not really respectable for older women. Men's styles changed much more slowly. Cotton replaced linen for shirts and underclothes and was much easier to wash. Boots rather than shoes were worn by men and women of all classes. The poor wore wooden clogs to work and had to make do with woollen shawls for warmth.

A MAN OF FASHION

This gentleman of about 1860 would never go out without his hat, cane and gloves. His jacket, waistcoat and trousers are a bit like a modern suit but were not then made from matching cloth. He is wearing a cravat around his neck which was the ancestor of the modern tie. Almost all men wore bushy whiskers between the 1840s and 1870s.

CHILDREN'S CLOTHES

This photograph shows the clothes of working-class children around 1890. They are all dressed for hard wear and tear. The girls have smocks to protect their dresses from stains and dust. Boys' clothes were usually made of tough corduroy or tweed. Almost everyone is wearing a hat. It was not respectable to go bare-headed.

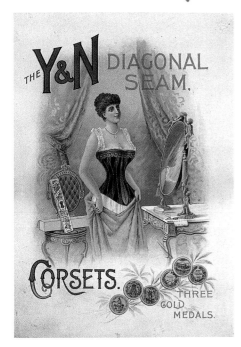

Ladies did not wash their hair very often so hats were an important fashion item and were always worn outdoors. Thousands of milliners were employed in making hats. Lace, ribbons and real bird feathers were used to decorate them.

Upper-class men wore shiny silk top hats. In the evening they could wear a folding 'opera hat' which collapsed so that it could go under the seat at a theatre. Middle-class men wore 'bowler' hats and working men wore soft, flat cloth caps. These were also worn by boys and sportsmen when cycling or shooting.

CORSETS

It was fashionable for women to have tiny waists so tight corsets were worn from the 1840s until 1914. Corsets made of whalebone or steel often crushed the insides and made breathing difficult so the wearer felt faint and dizzy. But women ignored doctors' advice not to wear them. Men also wore corsets for riding to help their posture.

LADIES' FASHIONS

These well-off ladies of the mid-century period are completely covered by their clothes from head to toe. Active work or exercise was impossible in clothes like these. They spent hours each day in dressing and changing, with separate outfits for morning, afternoon and evening, and for indoors and out. Most wealthy ladies had a personal maid whose main job was to look after their hair and clean and alter their clothes.

· WAS · RELIGION IMPORTANT?

Victorian Britain thought itself to be a Christian country and thousands of churches and chapels were built in this period. A third of all the time spent debating in Parliament was devoted to religious questions. Religious differences affected which sort of school children were sent to. There were strict laws to control what people could and couldn't do on Sunday. But the only time the government tried to count how many people actually went to church or chapel on a Sunday they discovered it was only 6.3 million – one in three!

A CHRISTIAN RULER

This painting of Queen Victoria presenting a Bible to an African king represents an event which probably never actually took place! But, even if the Queen didn't go around giving out Bibles in person, she and most British people thought they had a duty to send missionaries to countries where Christianity was unknown. Missionaries did found Christian communities and set up schools and hospitals throughout Africa, eastern Asia and the Pacific. By translating the Bible missionaries also increased Europeans' knowledge of African and Asian languages and customs.

A SHOCKING PICTURE

This painting of 'Christ in the House of His Parents' by Millais caused a storm of protest when it was first shown in 1850. Charles Dickens thought it was far too realistic and the people were all too ugly. It is full of religious symbols - the boy Christ's cut hand stands for the crucifixion, the dove is the Holy Spirit, the triangle represents the Trinity and the sheep are ordinary people who need guiding by religion.

STAINED GLASS

The most popular style for new churches was the gothic architecture of the Middle Ages. This meant an enormous demand for richly coloured stained-glass windows which showed scenes from the Bible or told stories about the lives of holy people. They were often put on the western or eastern side of churches for the most dramatic effects of light. The pieces of stained glass are held in place by a framework of lead.

Stained-glass window

 ## THE ROMAN CATHOLIC REVIVAL

After Britain became a Protestant country in the sixteenth century, people became deeply afraid of Catholics in case they supported plots or invasions by Catholic Spain or France. Until 1829, Catholics were forbidden to become MPs or judges. After that there was a Catholic revival, strengthened by the arrival of many Irish immigrants. By 1840, there were 700,000 Catholics in Britain and by 1911 there were over 1.7 million. A fine new Catholic cathedral was built at Westminster between 1896 and 1903.

THE SALVATION ARMY

This picture shows William Booth, who founded the Salvation Army in 1865. He is addressing a packed meeting. He wanted to reach out to the people who wouldn't normally come into a church and found that military-style bands and uniforms helped him to get their attention. William Booth actively campaigned against drink. He also encouraged people to emigrate to find better lives for themselves.

· D I D · PEOPLE · GO·TO·THE ·DOCTOR?·

During Victoria's reign more sick people than ever before benefited from medical care because there were more trained doctors and nurses and more hospitals and clinics. Laws were passed to stop people pretending to be doctors without proper qualifications. After 1865, women were also allowed to qualify as doctors. The introduction of anaesthetics in 1846 made surgery far less painful and the use of antiseptics cut down the risk of dying after an operation or from an infected wound. X-rays were discovered in 1895, which enabled doctors to see inside the body without surgery.

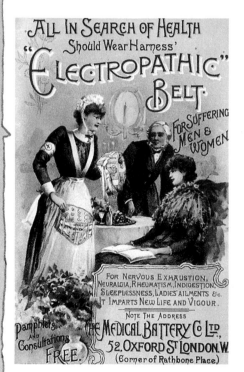

PILLS, POTIONS AND PATENT GADGETS

New medicines and methods of curing illnesses appeared every year. Before anaesthetics some doctors tried hypnotising their patients to spare them pain, others just gave them alcohol. Even doctors found it difficult to tell good new ideas from useless ones. This advertisement on the left claims to use the mysterious new power of electricity to treat a wide range of ailments. Coca-Cola was originally sold as a 'brain tonic'!

THE LADY WITH THE LAMP

This picture shows Florence Nightingale (seated in the middle) with a group of nurses at the training school she started at St Thomas's Hospital, London. She became famous for her work with the wounded during the Crimean War against Russia in 1854–6. She used to go round all the wards every night so her patients called her 'The Lady with the Lamp'.

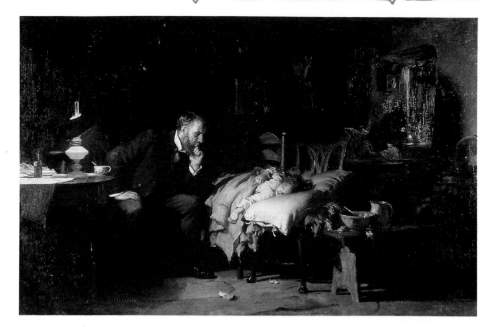

A SICK CHILD

Every Victorian parent could understand the situation in this painting immediately. Few families did not lose at least one child from illness or an accident. There were not many effective medicines to fight infections and most victims were saved by rest, good food and patient nursing. The rich could afford to send their sick children to hospitals but often preferred to nurse them at home because of the risk of catching illnesses from other patients.

 ## DENTISTRY

Dentistry, like surgery, became less painful thanks to anaesthetics. But it could still be very unpleasant – the newly invented dentist's drill was operated by pedal power and went very slowly! Many Victorian dentists had no professional training and this did not become compulsory until 1921.

Dentist's pliers

Scalpel

A CHILDREN'S WARD

The photograph above shows a light, airy ward for children at Guy's Hospital in London around 1900. This is a surgical ward where children came for operations. The toys were there to encourage them to play and get fit again afterwards. On the left are old brackets for holding gas lamps. These have been replaced by modern electric lighting. As late as 1900, 150 babies out of every 1,000 born died before their first birthday, many from common childhood diseases like measles or whooping cough. There were also special 'isolation' hospitals outside most big cities where people with highly infectious fevers were treated.

WHO·RULED·THE·COUNTRY?

At the beginning of Victoria's reign rich landowners were still the most powerful group in Parliament. In the 1840s, Sir Robert Peel became Prime Minister. He was one of the new middle-class politicians whose family had made a fortune in business. By the 1890s a few working men were being elected to Parliament with the help of trade unions. MPs were not paid until 1911 so poor people could only get elected with union support.

REIGNING, NOT RULING

This painting shows Victoria when she became Queen, aged eighteen, in 1837. Like the present Queen she had to pass the laws wanted by the Prime Minister and Parliament rather than what she might have wanted herself. Victoria was strongly opposed to giving women the vote!

A WISE ADVISER

This painting shows Albert, the German prince who married Victoria. Although he was her husband this did not make him King and he was known as the Prince Consort. Victoria almost always followed his wise advice. After he died in 1861 Victoria reigned alone for 40 years.

TWO GREAT RIVALS

Gladstone (right, standing) was leader of the Liberal Party and became Prime Minister four times. His greatest rival was Disraeli (left, sitting), leader of the Conservative Party, who was Prime Minister twice. This picture shows a debate in the House of Commons in the 1870s. Gladstone was always trying to cut taxes and improve conditions in Ireland. Disraeli got control of the Suez Canal for Britain and made Victoria Empress of India.

Close of the Poll, FIRST DAY.			
	Henniker.	Vere.	Shawe.
Woodbridge - - -	255	264	226
Ipswich - - -	513	529	348
Needham-Market - -	165	168	94
Saxmundham - -	200	188	131
Framlingham - -	306	261	307
Halesworth - -	340	319	293
Beccles - - -	365	348	395
MAJORITY In Favor of the Blues, - 285 !			
WOODBRIDGE, January 14, 1835.			

HOW THEY VOTED

This poster shows how electors in Suffolk towns voted in 1835. At that time people still had to say in public how they wanted to vote. This made it easy for landlords and employers to bully voters in favour of the MP they wanted. After voting became secret in 1872 this couldn't happen any more. If you add up how many votes each candidate got, you can see how few people had the right to vote.

VOTES FOR WOMEN!

These women are demonstrating for the right to vote – the suffrage. They were called suffragettes. They were willing to break the law by smashing windows to get publicity. In prison they went on hunger strike as a protest. Women finally got the vote in 1918 but only at the age of 30. From 1928 they could vote at 21 like men.

REFORMING PARLIAMENT

Parliament gradually extended the right to vote to more and more men, passing laws in 1832, 1867 and 1884. But even in 1914 one in four men failed to qualify for the vote because they didn't stay long enough at one address to register. The 1832 law gave big new cities like Birmingham and Manchester the right to elect MPs for the first time. In 1883, strict laws were passed against bribing voters. Other rules limited the amount that political parties could spend on elections so that poor candidates could have a fair chance.

WERE THERE ARTISTS IN VICTORIAN TIMES?

From the 1840s onwards Victorian artists found that they were in competition with a new invention – photography. For the first time in history it was possible to make accurate pictures of people, places and objects without drawing or painting. Many painters therefore chose to produce what the camera still couldn't. They did scenes with strong colour or lighting effects, scenes involving rapid movement or scenes of historical or imaginary events or people. A group of artists called the Pre-Raphaelites became famous for painting pictures about the Middle Ages.

ART ON SHOW

This painting, called 'Public Opinion', shows visitors at an exhibition making up their minds about a new painting. A rail has been put in front of the picture to protect it. A popular painting could make an artist very wealthy but it might take a whole year or more to paint. W.P. Frith got £4,500 for 'The Railway Station'(see page 9), equal to about ten years' income for a doctor. Some artists put their pictures on show and charged people to see them. Others got money from printers who sold cheap engraved versions of them. By 1900, most big cities had founded art galleries where local people could see paintings free of charge.

AN ARTIST IN HIS STUDIO

This painting, called 'The Sleepy Model' is in fact a self-portrait by the painter, W.P. Frith. The model was an Irish girl who sold oranges in the street. Frith, like most really successful artists, was well-trained and hard-working. His paintings were based on careful research and sketches. He also knew that his customers liked pictures of pretty girls. A painting like this, showing the artist at work, was a clever advertisement for his skill and thoroughness.

Fabric design by William Morris

 ## PHOTOGRAPHY

Photography was invented in France in 1826. The first photograph took eight hours to take! In 1835, Frenchman Jacques Daguerre invented the 'Daguerreotype', a sort of picture printed on metal. In 1840, the

Camera

Englishman W.H. Fox Talbot discovered how to print photographs on paper. The first flash picture was taken in 1850. The first cheap, simple camera which anyone could use easily was invented in 1888 by American George Eastman, the founder of the Kodak Company. Film on rolls was invented in 1889 and the first effective method of taking colour photographs was perfected in 1891.

ART AND DESIGN

This photograph shows the 'Honeysuckle Bedroom' at Wightwick Manor, which was designed by William Morris. He was one of the Pre-Raphaelite group but soon gave up painting in favour of interior decoration. He became a great expert at designing wallpaper, carpets and textiles. Many of his patterns are based on flowers, plants and birds. His firm sold high-quality goods to well-off people but Morris believed that everyone should have beautiful things in their homes. He was also famous as a poet and revived the art of printing beautiful books. William Morris wallpapers can still be bought today.

DID·PEOPLE GO·TO·THE THEATRE·IN VICTORIAN ·TIMES?·

During the early years of Victoria's reign going to the theatre was not really respectable. Actors and actresses would not have been welcome guests in many homes. Plays were often about robberies or murders. Audiences were sometimes rowdy and threw things at the stage. Opera, ballet and concerts by orchestras or choirs were much more acceptable to the middle and upper classes. The comic operas written by Gilbert and Sullivan were so successful that London's Savoy theatre was built just for them (1881). It was the first to have electric lighting.

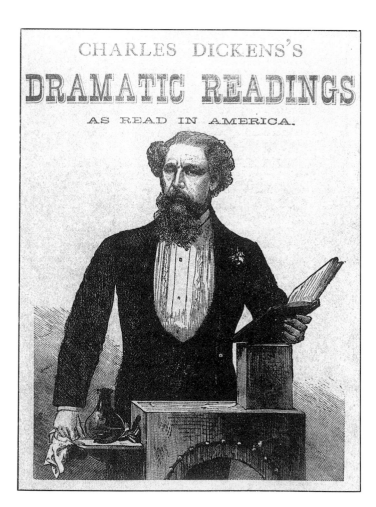

STREET ENTERTAINERS
Poor people enjoyed street entertainers who played musical instruments, juggled or did acrobatics. This man is going to escape after being tied up with a rope by a sailor. In the big cities, entertainers could live in one place and work in a different area each day. But most street entertainers were always on the move, from one country fair or race-meeting to the next. Life for them was very hard in winter when there were no fairs or races and people didn't want to stand around in the cold to watch them.

A KEEN THEATRE-GOER
The novelist Charles Dickens (1812–70) loved the theatre and went two or three times a week when he was young. He wanted to be an actor before he became a writer. When he became rich he built a tiny theatre in his house and put on plays to audiences of friends. He also gave brilliant readings from his novels in Britain and America. He used different voices for all the different characters.

THE GREATEST ACTRESS OF HER DAY

Ellen Terry (1847–1928) first acted on stage at the age of nine and gave her last performance aged 78. This portrait shows her as Lady Macbeth. In the play she never actually holds the crown over her head but the artist thought it would look good if she did!

MUSIC HALLS

The engraving below shows that in the cheap, noisy music hall there was often as much action in the audience as on stage. You can see how the performers are lit up by footlights. Music halls put on short scenes from plays rather than whole plays or else a series of acts by singers, acrobats or conjurors. Every big town had two or three music halls and London had dozens.

A KNIGHT OF THE THEATRE

The real name of Sir Henry Irving (1838–1905) was John Henry Brodribb! He was the first actor ever to be knighted for his work in the theatre. He made Shakespeare's plays popular with audiences after a long period in which they had been ignored. Irving often acted with Ellen Terry and toured the USA and Canada six times.

Sir Henry Irving and Ellen Terry

HOME ENTERTAINMENT

This brightly coloured toy theatre would have been given to a Victorian child as a Christmas or birthday gift. All the cardboard parts had to be cut out by hand.

WERE·THERE VICTORIAN SCIENTISTS?

The Victorian period was a great age of discoveries in science and technology. Geologists studying rocks and fossils showed that the earth was *much* older than people had ever thought it was. For the first time electricity was put to practical use – to send messages by telegraph and later to provide light for streets and homes and power for industry. The first plastics were invented – celluloid in 1870 and rayon in 1891. Industry also began to use new materials like rubber and aluminium. In 1835, Charles Babbage invented an 'analytical engine' which was the ancestor of the modern computer. It used punched cards and 50 cog wheels to do calculations. Schools and colleges also began to teach science.

ANGELS OR APES?
Charles Darwin (1809–82) wrote books explaining how living things had evolved from simpler creatures over millions of years. Many Victorians thought this theory of *evolution* contradicted the Bible. Darwin is drawn as an ape in this cartoon because people thought animals had been created separately and they couldn't believe that humans were related to chimpanzees!

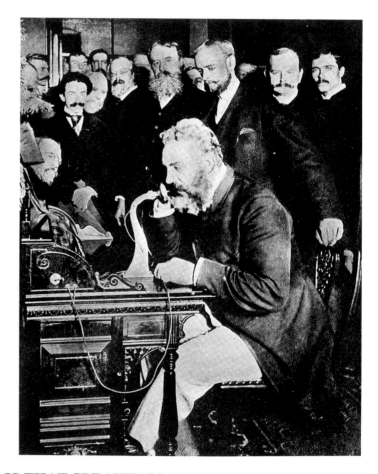

WHO IS THAT SPEAKING?
The first practical telephone was invented by the Scotsman Alexander Graham Bell in 1876. This picture shows Bell demonstrating his invention. He was an expert on teaching deaf people how to speak. He found out how to make a telephone as a result of an accident while he was mending a telegraph machine. Businesses were quick to see the value of Bell's invention.

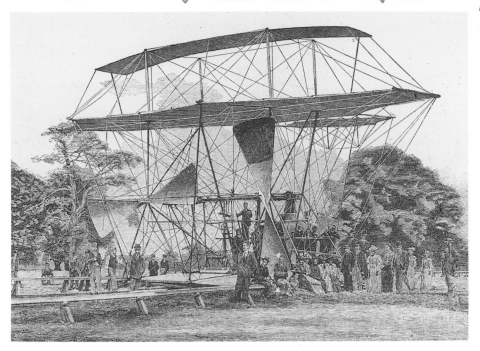

A FLYING MACHINE

Flying with balloons dates back to 1783. The Englishman Sir George Cayley (1773–1857) pioneered experiments with gliders and suggested the idea of propellers. In 1871, a Frenchman made a model plane powered by rubber bands which flew over 50 metres. But experimental flying machines like the one shown above were either too heavy or too fragile to work. The first successful manned, powered flight was made in the USA in 1903 by Orville Wright and watched by his brother Wilbur. It lasted twelve seconds and covered 36 metres – less than the length of a modern jumbo jet!

A TRIUMPH OF ENGINEERING

Isambard Kingdom Brunel (1806–59) was one of the greatest engineers of his age. This painting shows the railway bridge he designed to go over the River Tamar in Devon. Brunel also designed the Great Western Railway from London to Bristol and the *Great Britain*, the first all-iron steamship.

INVENTIONS FOR WORK AND HOME

Matches	1826
Morse code*	1837
Fireproof safe† Gummed envelopes	1844
Safety-pin*	1849
Singer sewing-machine*	1851

Typewriter

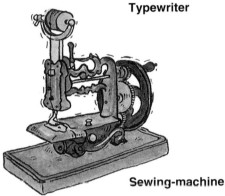

Sewing-machine

Pillar-box	1852
Corrugated iron†	1853
Dry-cleaning†	1855
Gas fires	1856
Typewriter*	1867
Toilet-roll*	1871
Cash register*	1879
Wrist watch†	1880
Electric iron*	1882
Skyscraper*	1885
Dish-washer*	1886
Electric torch	1891
Escalator*	1892
Zip-fastener*	1893
Safety razor*	1895
Vacuum cleaner Electric washing machine*	1901

* US invention

† French invention

The invention of railways and steamships made transport faster, safer and more reliable than ever before. On good roads stage coaches could average 12 kilometres an hour. In 1830, the first railway, from Liverpool to Manchester, carried passengers at over 30 kilometres an hour and by the 1850s at over 80 kilometres an hour.

The fastest sailing ships could cross the Atlantic in twelve days. Steamships could do it in under eight days. From the 1840s, steamships were used for passengers and mail, not because they were that much faster but because they didn't depend on the wind which meant they were more reliable. From the 1870s, more efficient engines meant that they had spare space for large cargoes.

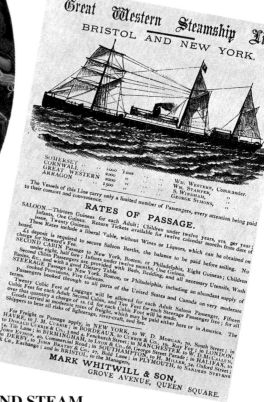

EMIGRATION

This painting, called 'The Last of England', shows a ship-load of emigrants leaving for Australia. The woman is clutching the tiny hand of a baby sheltered under her cloak. Most emigrants were young people who thought they had a chance of a better life in countries where there were more jobs and free land. Between 1815 and 1914, an estimated 15 million people left the British Isles. Many emigrants were encouraged to leave home by letters sent from friends who had already gone.

SAIL AND STEAM

The poster above advertises a trans-Atlantic steamship service. Because they did not depend on the wind, steamers could sail on fixed dates, but they still often used sails to save fuel! Passengers travelling on the cheapest fares had to bring their own bedding and wash-basins.

BUSINESS AND PLEASURE

By cutting transport costs, railways made it possible for businesses to buy their materials and sell their goods over much greater distances. Ordinary homes began to have food, clothes and other goods made hundreds or even thousands of kilometres away. Mail-order shopping became possible. Instead of being tiring and often dangerous, travel could be a pleasure. Railway companies offered holiday trips to the seaside. By the 1880s, trains had lighting, heating and corridors.

ON TIME!

This poster from 1845 advertises a horse-drawn bus service to the coast three times a week. As the railway system grew, transport companies which used horses had to think up new ways of getting business. In the end most turned to making deliveries or carrying passengers within towns because they couldn't compete with the speed and low fares of railways over longer distances.

MILESTONES IN TRAVEL

First London omnibus	1829	First air-brakes	1869
First passenger coaches	1830	First electric locomotive	
First electric signals	1856	First mountain funicular	1879
First train restaurant car		First trolley-bus	1882
First underground railway	1863	First electric tram	1888
First train sleeping cars	1865	First London – Brighton car rally	1896

THOMAS COOK AND SON

Thomas Cook (1808–92) was a printer and preacher who invented modern tourism. In 1841, he hired a train to take 570 passengers to hear a lecture against drinking. By 1851, he was organising trips to see the Great Exhibition and by 1856 he was offering tours around Europe. None of this would have been possible without cheap, reliable railway travel. In 1864, Cook's son, John, became his partner. From 1866 the firm began to book hotels as well as arranging travel. By the 1870s tourists could book trips to the Holy Land or down the Nile to see the pyramids.

WHAT·WAS ·LIFE·LIKE· IN·THE·ARMY ·AND·NAVY·?

Between 1815 and 1914 Britain only fought in one large war against a European country – the Crimean War (1854–6) in Russia. But the British army was fighting a small war in some part of the Empire almost every year. Soldiers were badly paid and until 1881 they could be punished by flogging. The Royal Navy was much more popular than the army with ordinary people. The British army was only a tenth as big as the French or German armies, but the navy was bigger than both of theirs added together. Little boys and girls were often photographed wearing sailor suits.

A GREAT DEFEAT

The army conquered large parts of Africa and Asia but did not win every battle! This painting (above) shows Isandlhwana where, in 1879, a force of 1,700 British soldiers was ambushed and killed by 20,000 Zulu warriors. The British recovered, however, and broke up the Zulu army within six months.

FURTHER, FASTER FIRE-POWER

Improvements in technology in the 1840s meant that the range of rifles increased from 200 metres to 1 kilometre. The invention of rifles that could be loaded from the back or side rather than down the barrel meant soldiers could fire five times faster and reload lying down.

Machine-guns, invented around 1850, could fire more bullets in a minute than 40 riflemen. Having machine-guns enabled the British army to conquer large parts of Asia and Africa with few troops. The Maxim gun (1884) was the first truly automatic machine-gun.

FROM SCARLET TO KHAKI

Bright uniforms helped generals follow the movements of troops in the smoke of battle. Khaki, first worn in India in 1857, offered much better camouflage.

OVER 11 KILOMETRES OF SHIPS!

In 1897, a naval review was held at Spithead to mark Queen Victoria's sixtieth year on the throne. This painting shows some of the 11 kilometres of ships which took part. They were still only about half of the Royal Navy's total strength of more than 300 ships. The rest were scattered over the seven seas from China to the Caribbean.

A TRIUMPHANT DISASTER

During the Crimean War (1854–6) the Light Brigade was ordered to charge a group of Russian guns. Their colonel led them against the wrong guns and the soldiers were shot at from three sides. Almost half of the 600 men were killed, but they were treated as heroes in Lord Tennyson's famous poem *The Charge of the Light Brigade*.

Maxim gun

Victoria Cross

THE VICTORIA CROSS

The Victoria Cross was established in 1856 and is the highest award given for bravery. The medals are made from the metal of captured Russian guns. Only 1,348 'VCs' have been awarded in over a century.

·GLOSSARY·

ANAESTHETIC A drug or gas used by doctors to stop a patient feeling pain, especially in operations.

ANTISEPTIC A substance that stops infections.

CAMOUFLAGE A way of disguising or hiding yourself. Camouflaged clothes blend into the surrounding country so you are more difficult to see.

COPPER A large tub, usually made of copper, in which water was boiled to wash dirty clothes.

CRAVAT A kind of scarf worn around the neck by men before ties were invented.

DIVIDEND A share of profit which is split up between people depending on how much they have put into the shop or business.

DUNCE A pupil who is slow at learning.

EMIGRANT Someone who leaves their country of birth to go abroad to live permanently.

EVOLUTION The theory that species of animals and plants developed over millions of years from simpler life forms rather than being created separately and never changing.

FLOGGING Beating with a whip or cane.

FULLER'S EARTH A type of clay, like a natural soap, used for washing grease out of textiles.

FUNICULAR A kind of railway built up steep slopes. The carriages are pulled up by a belt attached to a fixed engine.

GEOLOGIST A scientist who studies rocks.

GOTHIC A style of building using pointed arches which was popular in the Middle Ages.

GOVERNESS A woman teacher employed by a family to teach the children at home.

IMMIGRANT Someone who has arrived from another country to live.

IMPRESSIONIST PAINTING A style of art which began in France. It aimed to give an impression of how a scene was affected by the changing effects of light.

LOCOMOTIVE The engine part of a train which pulls the carriages along.

LODGER Someone who is not a member of the family who pays rent for a room in a family's house.

MANSION FLAT A large luxurious flat.

MILLINER Someone who makes women's hats.

MOTTO A saying to remind people of an important idea.

NUTRIENTS Substances in food which are necessary to keep a person healthy.

OMNIBUS Latin word meaning 'for all'. It was a horse-drawn carriage travelling along a set route which anyone could ride in if they paid a fare. 'Bus' is short for omnibus.

PATENT A legal document which bans other people from copying an inventor's idea.

PENSION Money people live on after they have retired.

PREFECT A senior pupil who is responsible for making sure the younger children behave.

SCULLERY A small room at the back of the house for washing dishes, dirty clothes, etc.

SLUM An area of very poor housing which is often overcrowded.

SMOCK An outer garment worn to keep clothes underneath clean.

SUFFRAGETTES Women who campaigned to get the vote.

TENEMENT Block of flats often found in Scottish cities.

TEXTILE Woven cloth used for curtains, bed linens, clothes, etc.

TROLLEY-BUS Type of bus which ran on rails.

X-RAYS A special type of photograph taken by doctors to see inside the body.

ZEPPELIN A huge cigar-shaped balloon with a cabin underneath for transporting passengers.

· I N D E X ·